IMPOLLUTABLE
POGO

DON'T TREAD ON ME

by

Walt Kelly

Simon and Schuster

SBN 671—20737—7
Library of Congress Catalog Card Number: 72-132022
Manufactured in the United States of America
By The Murray Printing Company, Forge Village, Mass.

6   7   8   9   10   11   12   13   14   15

In memory of
Joe Barnes,
who early on
understood freedom

Contents

AN EARLY FINAL THOUGHT

... The personal hummock in our common swamp is frail. The tough mind is very often an attempt to retain the property of self. If we identify with possessions and powers that are transient, how is it possible to scoff at the youth, who for at least this one young, blinding moment, realizes that these are not the things he yearns for?

We old grumps will remember that one of the drives of our youth was to "Make the world safe for democracy." Now, as goblins loom on every side, we are with George Washington. We cannot tell a lie. Youth looks at the Big Bomb, Big Government, Big Labor, Big Crime, Big Britches, and we must admit with him, in the words of a Pogo character, "We gotta make democracy safe for the world."

WALT KELLY, in the Milwaukee *Journal*,
February 22, 1970

Chapter 1

LOOKING AHEAD BEHIND
BY A NOSE

12

WE SENT HIM OUT FOR IT.

WONDER WHY **I** WAS SENT OUT FOR LUNCH ··· DON'T **THEY** WANT ANY? DO I LOOK **PALE**? IS I GOT **HALIOTOSIAS**? OR **ATHELETIC FEETS**?

YOU'LL RECALL, A FEW YEARS BACK, WE SUGGESTED A NEW CALENDAR ··· ONE WHICH HAD 365 DAYS PER YEAR OF **SOLID** OCTOBER?

SPLENDID!

1-5

THAT WOULD PLEASE THOSE WHO HAD ALL OF **OCTOBER** AS A **VACATION** ···

BUT YOU'D HAFTA BE FAIR ··· HOW 'BOUT THOSE WHO GOT **FEBRUARY**?

WELL, **THEY** IS STARTIN' IN HARD LUCK.

YEH, **I** DOUBT VERY MUCH THAT A SOLID YEAR OF **COMPLETE** FEBRUARY WOULD BE A BIG SELLER.

13

Chapter 2

WHICH VICE IS VERSA?

JUST TO DIMNISH **AIR-POLLUTION** YOU CAN'T DEMAND THAT PEOPLE STOP *BREATHIN'*···

WHY NOT?

IT'S A **AGE OLD HABIT**··· A REAL TRADITION···· PEOPLE DO IT IN THEIR *SLEEP* EVEN···· *EVER'BODY'S* ALWAYS **INHALIN'** AND **EXHALIN'**.

HA!

1-16

INHALIN' AND **EXHALIN'**! YOU COULD CUT THAT **RIGHT IN HALF**···

CUT OUT THE **INHALIN'**? OR THE **EXHALIN'**?

WELL, WE COULD LEAVE *THAT* DECISION TO A COMMITTEE··· OR TO A POPULAR VOTE.

LET'S SEE···· IF YOU *INHALED* AND DIN'T *EXHALE*··· OR UM·· VICE VERSA···· MMM ···· LESSEE NOW···

CHURCHY HERE IS BLOWN HIS BINNACLE ABOUT **AIR POLLUTION**.

YEAH··· *BREATHIN'* IS THE **ROOT** PROBLEM···

IT'S THE **INHALIN'** AND *EXHALIN'* THAT CAUSES TROUBLE···· PEOPLE SHOULD DO ONE OR THE OTHER···· *NOT BOTH!*

1-17

Chapter 3

FOUR BATS AND A BALL

23

24

Chapter 4

BARELY BEAR

Chapter 5

A HEAD IN A HOLE
AND VICE VERSA

33

Chapter 6

UNCLE BEANFELLOW IS DEAD SURE

38

Chapter 7

THE DRIVE-IN,
SELF-SERVICE MORTUARY

41

43

Chapter 8

A HAIR'S BREATH

Chapter 9

AN UNSPEAKABLE MINORITY

54

Chapter 10

TWENTY PERCENT OF ZERO
IS BETTER THAN
NOTHING

57

60

Chapter 11

THE CORRIDOR TO NOWHERE
IS A LONG HAUL

Chapter 12

THE PETTIFOGGERY OF SUBTERFUSION

68

Chapter 13

TWENTY YEARS,
A BED OF STONE AND THOU...
SINGING?

Chapter 14

JUSTICE IS BLIND, DEAF AND STONED

78

Chapter 15

HUNG UP
ON THE ECTOPLASTIC PHONE

Chapter 16

THE ROVER BOYS WOULD RATHER WRITHE

NOTHIN' TO IT... GETTIN' OUT OF HERE, I MEAN.

FAZBAZ!

ALL WE DO IS TEAR UP THE **BED SHEETS**, TIE 'EM TOGETHER AND SHINNY DOWN TO THE GROUND.

BRILLIANT!

HEY! SEND IN A SET OF SHEETS!

DO YA WANT THE **IRON ONES** OR THE **TIN**?

If you get cloth bed sheets, you'll tie them together, fasten them to the window~~~

~~~and escape by sliding down to the ground~~~

IN THAT CASE, JUS' GET ME A *ROPE*.

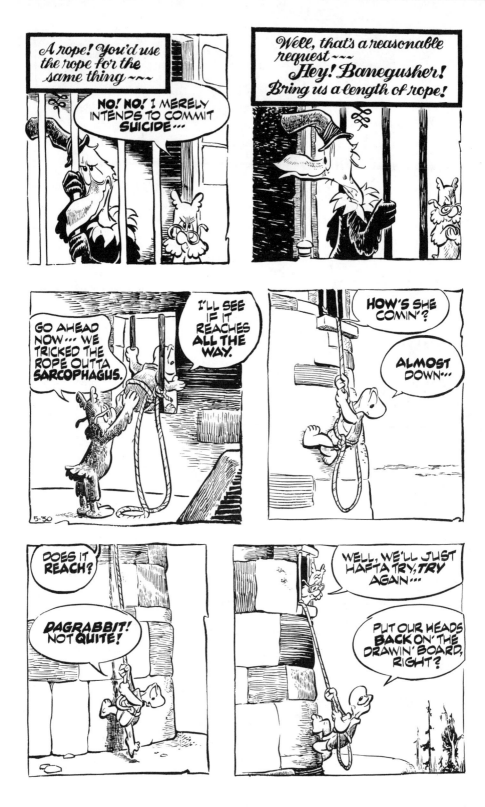

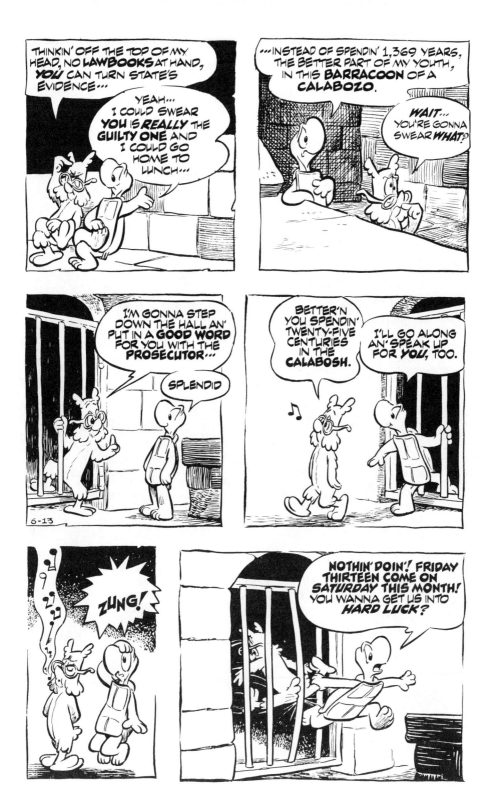

Chapter 17

WRONG NUMBER:
NOBODY HERE BUT US

96

Chapter 18

STEADILY UPWARD,
ONWARD AND OVER

Chapter 19

A CLEARING IN THE FOREST
OF THE MIND

Chapter 20

A CLEARING IN A JUGULAR VEIN

THE WILD BLOWN YONDER

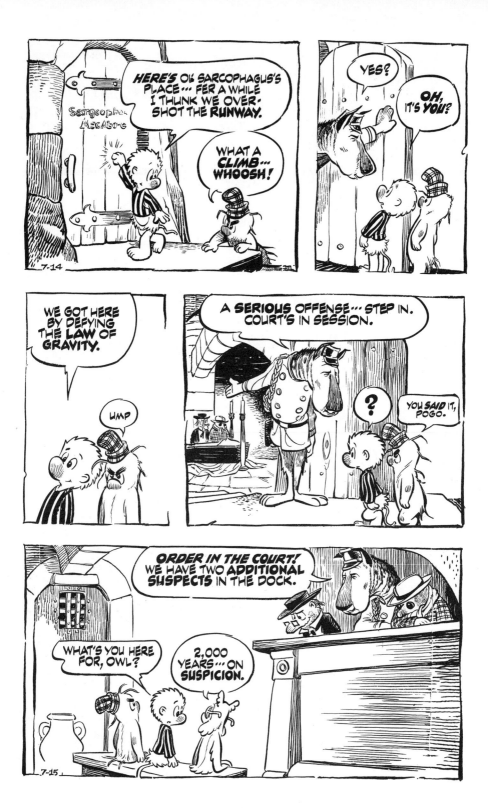

7-16

116

117

120

Chapter 22

ALL'S WELL THAT ENDS

NOW THERE MUST BE AMONGST US A DOZEN *PUBLIC SPIRITED CITIZENS* WITH *PUBLIC SPIRITED TAILS WHICH* THEY'D BE HAPPY TO *CONTRIBUTE* TO *ADD* ON TO THE ROPE --- *SPEAK UP!*

DEACON! YOU GOT A *NICE LONG TAIL* WHAT YOU SHOULD CONTRIBUTE TO *HUMANITY*...

But---

7-30

If you want to add to the rope, Pogo's tail is young, vibrant, flexible --- brimming with the strength of youth --- Here, examine the product --- a gem!

HEY!

MM --- BY JING! BEAUTIFUL.

Not like mine --- brittle with care and age.

WE'LL USE IT!

Hey --- I gave you the wrong --- Hey!

123

124

YEA, THE INDUCIVE, INDUCTEOUS AND INDUCTIBLE **INDUCIAE** MAY YET BE THE REPOSOIR OF OUR REPOUSSAGE ·······**OR**, ALTERNATELY, THE **REPLEVIABLE REPLEVY.**

YES, THE PENULTIMATE PERQUISITES ARE **PERENNIAL**···

8-5.

AND PRAGMATICAL IN THE JUDICIAL GENERALITIES.

INDUBITABLY IN THE EXQUISITES, *RIGHT?*

RIGHT! *RIGHT!*

RIGHT!

HOW MANY OF HIM WAS THERE?

RIGHT!

RIGHT

RIGHT

RIGHT